Into the Unknown

Major Powell's River Journey

Text by Peter Anderson
Illustrations by Tom McFarland

For Young Readers—from Falcon Press

Highlights from American History
The Lewis and Clark Expedition
Flight of the Nez Perce
Into the Unknown: Major Powell's River Journey

Interpreting the Great Outdoors
The Fire Mountains
The Tree Giants
Oregon Wildflowers
Arizona Wildflowers
California Wildflowers

Falcon Press distributes a wide variety of books and calendars, including children's books. You can get a free catalog by writing Falcon Press, P.O. Box 1718, Helena, MT 59624, or calling 1-800-582-2665. You can also get announcements of future books in the Highlights from American History series and the Interpreting the Great Outdoors series.

Copyright © 1992 by Falcon Press Publishing Co., Inc. Billings and Helena, Montana.

Design, editing, typesetting, and other prepress work by Falcon Press, Helena, Montana. Printed in Singapore

Library of Congress Number 91-58884
ISBN 1-56044-133-X

Journey into the Unknown

By 1869, much of the American West had already been explored. Lewis and Clark had blazed a trail into the Pacific Northwest. Fur trappers had roamed the Rocky Mountains. Wagon trains had rumbled across the Great Plains. Prospectors had rushed West to search for gold. And railroad tracks had just stretched all the way across the country.

But there were still blank spaces on the map—wild lands west of the Rockies that no one knew much about. Among the most remote and mysterious of these were the canyons of the Green and Colorado rivers. No one knew for sure what lay in the deep gorges these rivers carved through the plateau country of Wyoming, Colorado, Utah, and Arizona.

Some people said the steep canyon walls—more than a mile high in places—came right down to the river's edge. Others talked of waterfalls bigger than those at Niagara. Some warned of giant whirlpools that could swallow a boat. And there were Indians who described a place where the Colorado River ran into the mouth of a huge cave and disappeared.

On May 24, 1869, ten men gathered along the banks of the Green River in southwestern Wyoming Territory. They intended to travel by boat through these wild and mysterious canyons. The muddy river was swollen with melted snow. It twisted like a giant question mark through low bluffs and broken badlands toward a distant range of snowcapped mountains. To the south, the river poured into the mouth of a canyon and began its long journey into the unknown.

The Major and His Men

A crowd of spectators cheered as the ten men pushed their boats into the current that day. The men steered with giant sweep oars, trying their best to swerve around sandbars and gravel banks.

Leading the way in the smallest of the four boats was a one-armed Civil War veteran named John Wesley Powell. Major Powell was an adventurous geologist and explorer. At the age of 22, he had rowed a boat down the Mississippi River, from Illinois all the way to New Orleans.

Growing up on the edge of the frontier in Illinois, Powell became interested in nature at an early age. Despite discouraging words from his father, who wanted him to become a minister, Powell continued to explore and study the natural world. Later he met a wonderful teacher who took him on field trips, helped him learn about the forests of the

Midwest, and taught him to respect the Indians who had once lived there. Inspired by this man, Powell decided to become a teacher himself.

Then came the Civil War. Powell joined the Union Army, working his way up to be an officer. During the Battle of Shiloh, a bullet shattered his right arm. Three days later, the arm had to be amputated below the elbow. But as soon as Major Powell recovered, he returned to battle. Despite his pain, he refused to let his handicap get in the way.

After the war, Powell returned to teaching and began leading field trips into the Rocky Mountains. On one trip, he met a young trapper and guide named Jack Sumner. This man led Powell to the headwaters of the Colorado (then known as the Grand) River. And he told Powell of canyons farther west that had never been explored.

Now, only a few years later, Sumner and a shaggy mountain man named Bill Dunn were steering Major Powell's boat, the *Emma Dean,* toward those very canyons. Behind them came *Kitty Clyde's Sister,* piloted by two former soldiers, George Bradley and Powell's moody brother Walter. Bradley was as tough as a badger. And having grown up in a New England fishing village, he knew a lot about boats.

Behind them, rowing the *No Name,* was Oramel Howland, a newpaper printer and editor from Colorado, and his soft-spoken younger brother Seneca. With them was Frank Goodman, an English adventurer. Goodman had arrived at Green River several days earlier and had volunteered to come along.

Bringing up the rear was fun-loving Andy Hall, a former scout and mule-driver, and Billy Hawkins, a cheerful young man who would be the group's cook. They rowed the *Maid of the Canyon.*

Ten men. Four boats. The crowd of spectators watched Major Powell and his crew drift toward those unknown lands. Some said the ten men would never be seen again.

Whitewater Thunder

Major Powell knew there were dangers ahead. To prepare for the journey, he had talked with trappers, Indians, and some of the few settlers who lived in this vast, unmapped region. As a geologist, he was thrilled by their descriptions of the deep canyons that lay ahead. With any luck, the river might have sliced its way down to some of the oldest rocks on the continent.

But Powell also knew there would be rough waters in the deep canyons—so rough that ordinary boats might not survive them. So he had boats specially made of sturdy oak. The three larger boats each came with a set of oars, more than one hundred feet of rope, and special storage compartments in the front and back to keep supplies dry. These boats would carry most of the tools and the rations—flour, sugar, beans, dried apples, salt pork, slabs of bacon, rice, coffee, and tea. The major hoped he had enough food to last ten months if necessary. Powell's boat, the *Emma Dean,* was smaller and lighter. It was designed to be the rescue boat.

On May 30, the walls of the first canyon began to rise around them. Here in this red-walled canyon they called Flaming Gorge, the river was as smooth as ice. They swirled past a huge sandstone tower honeycombed with tiny caves in which hundreds of swallows had made their nests.

But soon the river began to narrow. Now the canyon walls rose higher and came right down to the water. The men could hear the thunder of the first rapids ahead. As big rocks began to choke

the river channel, the *Emma Dean* led the way. Dunn and Sumner manned the oars. Major Powell bellowed directions as they plunged into a deep trough and rode up on the billowing waves. Their cheers echoed off the canyon walls as they slid into the quiet water below.

One by one, the other boats followed. The men laughed and hollered as they barreled through the waves to the quiet whirlpool below their first stretch of whitewater. Having survived one rapid, they were ready for more. If they had known what lay ahead, they would never have been so eager.

On June 8, the men entered a steep, dark canyon and saw a terrifying sight. Gloomy black rocks surrounded the rushing foam of the river as it poured over a sudden waterfall, crashed into piles of boulders, and disappeared around a bend. Shouting to be heard over the roar of the falls, Major Powell ordered Dunn and Sumner to row to shore. He told Dunn to use signal flags to wave the other boats ashore while he walked farther downstream to scout the rapid. Maybe there was a way to carry the boats around, Powell thought as he scrambled among the rocks.

Then he heard someone yell. Looking back upstream, he could see Frank Goodman and the Howland brothers straining on the oars of their boat. They hadn't been able to pull over in time. Now they struggled to straighten the *No Name*, which had spun sideways in the current. But it was too late. A wave surged over the boat, washing the oars loose. The *No Name* tumbled out of control and smashed into a boulder. Clinging to pieces of the shattered boat, the three men disappeared around a bend in the canyon. They gasped for air in the raging foam.

7

Disaster at the Falls

Running along the riverbank, Major Powell rounded the bend just in time to see Goodman struggling to pull himself out of the current and onto a sharp rock. Nearby, Oramel Howland had washed onto a small island. Thinking fast, Oramel grabbed a long driftwood pole and pushed it toward Goodman. The desperate Englishman grabbed onto it with what little strength he had left, and Howland pulled him ashore. Meanwhile, Seneca, who had washed up on a pile of rocks in the middle of the river, swam over to the island.

Farther upstream, the rest of the crew used ropes to lower the rescue boat over the first big drop. Sumner was on board. He rowed out into the whitewater, aiming for the tip of the island. The strong current threatened to sweep him past, but he dug in. The long oars bent with each powerful stroke. At the last possible moment, the Howlands were able to grab the boat and pull it onto the island.

Sumner rowed the *Emma Dean* back across the river into calmer water. The rest of the crew welcomed the four men as if they had just returned from a voyage around the world. But there had been losses. One boat was shattered. Two thousand pounds of provisions and tools were gone. The shipwrecked men had lost all their personal belongings. Little wonder the men named this part of the river Disaster Falls.

After the rescue, the men were tense. Major Powell criticized Oramel Howland for ignoring Dunn's signal flags. Howland claimed that he had never seen a signal. Had Dunn forgotten to give one? As the campfire flickered that night, the dark walls of the canyon seemed especially gloomy. Below them, the men could hear the roar of another rapid.

For the next six days, the crew continued to struggle through

this place they named Lodore Canyon. In several places, they lined the boats around dangerous rapids. This meant they unloaded the boats and tied ropes to the bows and sterns. Half the men tugged on the bowlines, pulling the boats through the great waves. The other half let out rope from the rear, making sure to hold the sterns straight in the current.

Sometimes the rapids were too steep to line the boats. Then the men had to carry their boats and freight along the rocky shore. Their shoes tore and their feet blistered. Their hands swelled and were burned by the ropes. Their backs bent under the heavy loads. They progressed only a couple miles a day.

When the men tried to row through the rapids, their boats were battered. Almost every day someone capsized. At the very least, someone was thrown overboard. And their supplies were soaked. The bacon went bad, the beans sprouted, and the flour spoiled. Already their rations were running dangerously low.

Up in Flames

To make matters worse, wild game was scarce. Only a few mountain sheep were sighted now and then, and as Bradley said, they stayed up on the canyon walls "where a squirrel would hardly climb." And each night the crashing sound of the waves echoed through the men's dreams.

Still, there were brighter moments. In camp, they had time to relax—making moccasins, playing cards, reading or writing, mending clothes, or just catching up on some sleep. Sometimes, Walter Powell's loud, deep voice could be heard ringing through the canyon. He loved to sing, and his lively ballads entertained the crew.

Everyone shared the camp chores—hunting, drying out supplies, gathering firewood. But it was young Billy Hawkins who did most of the cooking. His cheerful call at mealtime helped to brighten spirits.

One day, as he was cooking supper, a whirlwind spun up the canyon.

It spread his campfire into the surrounding willow trees. Then another gust fanned the flames. Soon everything was burning. Grabbing what they could, the men ran for the river. Walter Powell dove into the river with his mustache on fire. Bradley howled as his ears got scorched. And Billy Hawkins stubbed his toe, fell into the river, and lost kettles, bake ovens, and all of their plates, knives, forks, and spoons.

The flames raged as the men piled onto the boats. They had to cut loose into a rocky rapid. There was no time to scout, no time for signals. The boats banged against one another and the men flailed with the oars as they swerved through a maze of rocks.

Meanwhile, Major Powell happened to glance down from the top of a ridge where he had gone exploring. He could see his men rowing through the waves below camp, but he couldn't see the fire. Where were they going? Scrambling down a rocky slope, he rushed back to the river. He found his crew pulling the boats onto a beach below the rapid. Only then did he realize what had happened.

A Seat-of-the-Pants Rescue

Sometimes the other men wondered why Major Powell spent so much time exploring around the river. After all, they were running low on supplies. Shouldn't they travel as far as possible each day? The other men didn't understand Major Powell's passion for knowledge.

But this strange land of bare rock, dwarfed trees, and deep canyons was unlike any place Major Powell had ever seen. As a biologist, he wanted to learn about the plants and animals living in the area. As a geologist, he wanted to understand the rock layers. And as an explorer, he wanted to map the river and its canyons.

So he spent days scrambling across narrow ledges, up rocky slopes, and through the cracks in canyon walls. Although he only had one arm, there were few places he wouldn't climb. He was a cautious man on the river. He rarely chose to run a dangerous rapid if there was a way to line or carry the boats around it. But he was willing to take chances when it came to climbing and exploring.

One day, Major Powell and George Bradley went out to climb the west wall of the canyon. After climbing over a narrow ledge high above the river, Bradley heard a shout below him.

Major Powell was trapped. Standing on a narrow shelf of rock, he had been able to jam a foot into a narrow crack and pull himself partway up a sheer rock face. But now, no matter how much he strained and stretched, he couldn't reach the next handhold. The only way to go back was to let go and jump down to the ledge. But if he missed the ledge, he would fall eighty feet.

Bradley scrambled out onto a nearby rock, but he couldn't get close enough to help. By now, Powell's legs were shaking. His heart was pounding. His fingers were beginning to cramp. Bradley needed something to reach down to the Major, but he was surrounded by nothing but rock. So he tore off his pants and lowered them down. If Major Powell could just grab on....

Powell's whole body was shaking. He had only one chance to save himself. He let go. He felt like he was falling, but at the last instant he clutched onto the dangling pantleg. Bradley pulled. And pulled. Finally Major Powell rolled onto the rock ledge with him—exhausted, gasping for breath, and grateful to be alive.

Trading with the Indians

Gradually, the river emerged from the dark-walled canyons the men had been traveling through for many days. They drifted past antelope feeding in green meadows and cottonwood groves filled with birds. They passed through several more canyons. Sometimes they had to row through rapids, but these were nowhere near as bad as the ones in Lodore. Maybe, as Bradley thought, the roughest waters were behind them.

On June 28, they reached the mouth of the Uinta River, a tributary that flows into the Green River from the northwest. Major Powell knew of a Ute Indian village about forty miles up the Uinta. There, for the first time on the journey, the crew might be able to send letters home to families and loved ones. Powell sent his brother Walter and Andy Hall off with the mail.

Meanwhile, Major Powell gathered up items to trade—coffee, tobacco, cloth. He had enjoyed previous experiences trading with the Indians. He

respected them and was interested in their customs and languages. As a result, the Indians knew and liked Powell. The Piutes called him "Kapurats," which means "one arm off."

On July 2, Hawkins, Goodman, and Major Powell followed Hall and Walter Powell along the Uinta River toward the Ute village. With any luck, they would be able to trade for enough supplies to get them through the canyons ahead.

But the Utes were also low on supplies. They wouldn't be able to harvest their crops for another month. Major Powell met with Tsauwiat, an ancient Ute chief who was thought to be more than one hundred years old. They smoked, talked, and finally worked out a trade.

Along with two Indian escorts, Hall, Hawkins, and the Powell brothers returned on horseback to the river with three hundred pounds of flour. Frank Goodman never came back. He had seen enough of the river and had decided to move on. Maybe it was for the best. Now there was one less mouth to feed.

An Unforgettable Stew

While Powell and his party visited the Indians, the rest of the men waited by the river. For several days, the hot sun beat down on them. Clouds of gnats swarmed over their bodies. The fishing and hunting were terrible.

They were relieved when Powell returned and they could get going again. And they were thrilled to discover a garden on an island downstream. Major Powell figured the garden belonged to a hunter and trader he had met the previous winter. But after a month without fresh vegetables, no one cared who the owner was. They gathered armloads of young beets, turnips, and potatoes. The vegetables were too small to eat, but the men figured they could boil the leaves.

Several miles downriver, the crew pulled onto a sandy beach. Hall threw everything into a big pot and made an unforgettable stew— unforgettable for all the wrong reasons. Everyone got sick! Major Powell thought the potato leaves caused the illness. Hall thought he just hadn't cooked the stew long enough. Sumner decided he would never rob a garden again.

The river was smooth here, but the men were miserable. With aching stomachs, they drifted beneath a scorching sun. Heat waves rose from the craggy rocks and rippled the sky. Hardly anything grew along the banks. There wasn't a blade of grass in sight. The occasional caw of a raven seemed to be the only sign of life in this empty land they called the Canyon of Desolation.

As they drifted farther into the canyon, the heat got worse. Even soaking wet in the middle of the river, they felt like they were in an

oven. The wind blew clouds of sand through camp. Even Bradley, who rarely complained, said it was as close to hell as anything he'd known.

But for Bradley, the worst of Desolation Canyon was yet to come. As the sandstone walls began to rise around the men once again, they heard the thunder of more rapids ahead. When they dropped into one of them, a wave crashed over Bradley's boat and washed him into the river. His head was buried in the water, and his foot was caught underneath the seat of the boat. Somehow Bradley managed to grab the edge of the boat with one arm. Maybe he could pull himself in. Smashing through wave after wave, his boat was headed for a rocky cliff. Then Walter Powell grabbed the oars and spun the boat past the cliff. In the quiet water below it, he hauled Bradley in.

The Colorado at Last

Desolation Canyon and then Gray Canyon just downstream were hard on the men and their equipment. Boats were cracked. Oars were lost or broken. Worst of all, the food supplies were damaged. Much of the flour had gotten wet and moldy, and several sides of bacon had spoiled in the heat.

At least the river was calm again. Below Gray Canyon, it swung lazily through broken gray bluffs. Then it meandered into yet another canyon whose towering sandstone walls changed color as the sun moved across the sky—from brown to red to orange in the early morning, to a light tan in the middle of the day, to orange and red and even purple at dusk.

But as the sun went down, these next two rainbow-colored canyons, which they called Labyrinth and Stillwater, were deep and dark. Eerie silhouettes of stone carved up the sky. At times, the quiet was unsettling. Finally, on July 16, the boats rounded a bend and the canyons opened up onto a view the men had been waiting for. Here, finally, was the junction of the Green and Colorado rivers.

Just below this junction, Major Powell and his men camped for three days, taking the time to patch up their cracked boats with pine pitch. They tried pouring the flour through a mosquito net to sift out the mold, but they still had to throw away 200 pounds. One night, during a dinner of musty bread and spoiled bacon, the men talked of all the foods they missed. Major Powell noticed Hawkins down by the boats tinkering with the navigational equipment. He asked the young cook what he was doing, and Hawkins said he was trying to find the latitude and longitude of the nearest pie!

For a few days, only the song of the canyon wren broke the silence in this strange land of rock castles. But that soon changed. Several miles downstream, the whitewater thunder returned, and for the next fifty miles or so, the roar of rapids rarely let up. The boats were hammered. Often, the waves were too big to row through. Even lining the boats was risky.

So in the fierce canyon heat, the men unloaded the boats and made trails along the rocky shores. Staggering under heavy loads, they walked—forever, it seemed—through this place they called Cataract Canyon.

It was hard to imagine that the rapids could get any worse. Still, some began to wonder if they would come to a place where the river was impassable...a place where vertical canyon walls came right down to the water...a place where there was no going forward, no climbing out, and no turning back.

A Canyon of Rare Beauty

Broiled by the sun, whipped by the rapids, and exhausted by the portages, Major Powell and his men plunged deeper into Cataract Canyon. As the canyon walls got higher and the hunting and fishing got worse, they thought more and more about their limited rations. At night they feasted in their dreams. In the morning, they woke up hungry.

Hunger and fatigue added to the tension they felt about what lay ahead—and the tension they felt with one another. Even though they were both reasonable, level-headed men, Oramel Howland and Major Powell had not gotten over the mishap at Disaster Falls. Powell still blamed Howland for losing the boat and supplies. Howland resented it. They argued often.

Fortunately, the crew's luck began to change for the better. On July 27, Sumner shot two bighorn sheep, which yielded a welcome feast. Then, the next day, they came to the end of Cataract Canyon.

Downstream, the men floated into a canyon more beautiful than any they had seen yet. They passed giant caves carved out of the sandstone by wind and water. They saw bright splashes of green—shady glens and waterfalls tucked away in the side canyons that fed into the river. They decided to call this place Glen Canyon.

Despite the peaceful beauty of Glen Canyon, Powell and his crew were anxious to reach the junction where the San Juan River flowed into the Colorado. They had heard rumors of a settlement there. But they were disappointed. At the mouth of the muddy San Juan, the riverbanks were deserted. The men were greeted only by the sound of crickets.

For Major Powell, this was an important landmark in mapping the river. With their surveying instruments, the men were able to estimate how far they had come. But some of the men cared more about how fast the food was disappearing. They thought it was a waste of time to spend several days mapping and taking readings near the mouth of the San Juan.

Wet, Tired, and Hungry

Even though Major Powell wanted to make the most of this exploration, he realized his crew was worn out and dejected. Half-naked, bearded, and skinny, the men grew weaker everyday.

As they approached the mouth of yet another canyon on August 5, the rocks began to change. There were harder layers of sandstone and limestone, like those they had seen in Cataract Canyon. Major Powell knew that harder rocks meant rougher water ahead. How much more could they take?

Soon the smooth, polished canyon walls rose almost three quarters of a mile high. Here in Marble Canyon, as the men called it, the river was slicing its way back in time. The farther the men went, the older the rock layers got. And as the rocks got older, the waves got bigger.

By now, the crew had less than a month's worth of food left. Meals were bleak—mostly coffee and biscuits. As the canyon narrowed, leaving only a slit of sky above them, they rode the waves deeper into the shadows.

The expedition was headed into the deepest gorge they had seen yet—the Grand Canyon. Great tilted masses of black rock appeared at the water's edge. Here were the ancient rocks that Major Powell had hoped to find. But for now, he had little chance to appreciate them.

Huge gray clouds piled up above the canyon rims, which rose more than a mile above them. Then it began to rain. For days it rained. A thousand streams rushed down off the canyon walls. The men had trouble finding places to camp, especially places where there was shelter from the rain. Their clothes were almost completely shredded and torn, and they had only a few blankets. Even when the men could find driftwood, the rain put out their fires. All they could do was huddle against the dark rocks and wait. But the mornings were cold, and the sliver of sky above them seemed to get smaller everyday. If there was a place where the earth swallowed the river, it couldn't be far away.

Three Want Out

By August 21, the worst seemed to be over. Downriver, the men could see where the hard granite disappeared and the softer limestone began. The canyon opened up until the men were floating under a wide swath of blue sky. They felt as though they were escaping from prison.

But six days later, the river swung to the south and led them into a stretch of canyon that was as dark and scary as any they had seen. The hard black rocks were back, and so were the rapids. The river crashed into the left bank of the canyon, tore through a channel choked with boulders, raged back to the right, and then vanished around the bend.

The only hope, it seemed, was to line the boats around the rapids. But how? Craggy granite cliffs flanked the river on both sides.

Major Powell spent the afternoon trying to find a route through the rocks, but he failed. The crew would have to row. If they made it over the first big drop, there would be other rapids around the bend. No one knew how many. One thing they did know was that they had only enough food to last five more days.

After dinner that night, Oramel Howland told Powell that he had decided to leave the expedition. He, his brother Seneca, and William Dunn wanted to try walking out of the canyon. Plunging back into the rapids with only five days' worth of food just seemed too risky. They would rather take their chances on land.

Powell said nothing about Howland's decision to the other men. Unable to sleep that night, he thought about how foolish the plan seemed. Judging from the stars and what his surveying instruments told him, Powell figured they might be eighty or ninety river miles from the nearest settlement. If they kept on by boat, at least part of the journey would be through smooth water. If the Howlands knew this, Powell thought, maybe they would reconsider.

He drew a map in the sand, woke Howland, and showed him where he thought they were. Their talk was brief. Howland had made up his mind.

Major Powell began to wonder. Had he made the right decision? The thunder of the rapids below camp seemed to grow louder and louder.

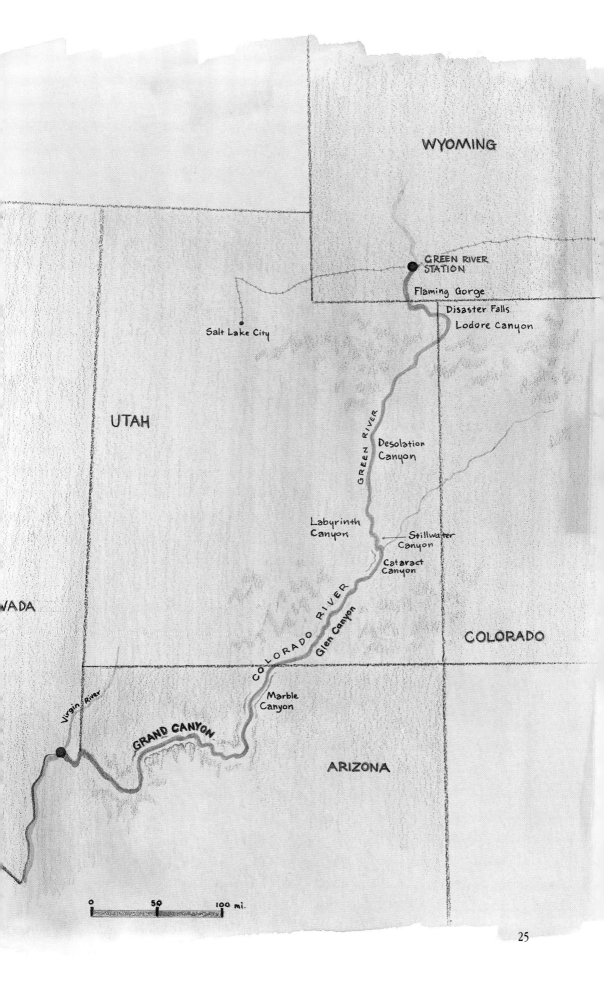

WYOMING

GREEN RIVER
STATION

Flaming Gorge

Disaster Falls

Lodore Canyon

Salt Lake City

UTAH

Green River

Desolation
Canyon

Labyrinth
Canyon

Stillwater
Canyon

Cataract
Canyon

COLORADO RIVER

Glen Canyon

COLORADO

VADA

Virgin River

Marble
Canyon

GRAND CANYON

ARIZONA

0   50   100 mi.

Sad Farewells

All night long, Major Powell paced up and down a sandy path by the river. Maybe the others were right. Maybe it was foolish to keep going with so little food. But the idea of walking out of the canyon had its problems, too. The canyon walls were steep. Finding a path to the rim might be difficult. It would be hot and dry, and water would be hard to find.

As the stars moved across the sky, Powell thought about the rapids they would face in the morning. They were big—as big as any he had seen—but he thought they could get through them. And the thought of leaving part of the canyon unexplored after having come this far was unacceptable. He would push on down the river. He woke his brother Walter, who agreed to stay with him. He woke Billy Hawkins. He woke Sumner, Bradley, and Hall. They all agreed to run the river.

The next morning, the men gathered for the usual breakfast of coffee and biscuits. They were somber and quiet, like people at a funeral. Only the thunder of the rapids broke the silence. Seneca Howland tried briefly to convince William Dunn and his brother to continue on the river, but he didn't change their minds. They had seen enough of the black rocks. Out of loyalty to his brother, Seneca decided to walk out, too.

Major Powell offered the men their share of the remaining coffee and flour, but Dunn and the Howlands refused. They planned to take three guns with them, and they thought they would be able to shoot wild game on the high plateaus.

Since only five of his crew members remained, Major Powell decided to take the two larger boats and leave the *Emma Dean* behind. Standing above what became known as Separation Rapids, the nine men sadly shook hands and said their farewells. Some even wiped away tears. Each group thought the other had made the wrong choice.

Dunn and the Howlands watched from a rocky crag overhanging the river as the two boats dashed into the tumbling waters. The oarsmen rowed furiously, but soon the waves were too big. All the boatmen could do was hold on as one boat and then the next slammed into a wall of white foam and disappeared around the bend.

A Terrible Dunking

When both boats had made it through Separation Rapids, the men fired guns to let Dunn and the Howlands know they were safe. Major Powell hoped the three might reconsider and follow in the *Emma Dean*. But the others never came.

So Powell and his remaining crew pushed on. About six miles downstream, they encountered a rapid that looked impossible to run. They would have to line the boats through. While some of the others let out the rope attached to the stern of his boat, Bradley was at the oars, trying to guide it to the head of a falls. Then the stern line snapped. The current ripped the boat loose. Bradley struggled to keep the boat straight.

Meanwhile, Powell and Sumner, who had been unable to hang onto the bowline, tried in vain to catch Bradley's boat before it slipped over the edge and into the whitewater. Bradley vanished.

Major Powell, Hawkins, and Hall jumped into the second boat,

hoping to rescue Bradley. But a huge wave buried their boat and washed them all overboard. Major Powell got a terrible dunking. The current held him underwater for what seemed like minutes. When he surfaced, the crashing waves barely gave him time to catch a breath. In the end, Bradley ended up rescuing the major.

On August 29, the men rowed out into a country of parched rolling hills. Now the gates of the Grand Canyon were closing behind them. The settlements on the Virgin River couldn't be far. The men began to celebrate. Walter Powell's songs drifted over the valley. Andy Hall tried to sing along with him, but his voice was so bad that Hawkins threatened to drown him.

That night, as the men camped under a vast canopy of blazing stars, their spirits soared. They talked of the canyons and the rapids. They talked of the future, of family and loved ones. And they hungrily dreamed of great feasts. But they also wondered about Dunn and the Howlands. Had they been able to find a way out of the canyon?

A Well-Deserved Feast

At daybreak, Major Powell and his crew were eager to get on down the river. Pulling hard on the oars, they made twenty-six miles by noon. At one point, they came upon a group of Indians. Speaking in the Ute tongue, Major Powell was able to coax them down to the river. He asked them about nearby settlements. If the Indians knew about them, they didn't say.

As afternoon wore on, the men continued to pull hard under a hot sun. Civilization couldn't be far now. Then someone noticed several people along the shore. They turned out to be fishermen from the Virgin River settlement—a Mr. Asa and his sons—and they stood beside a net full of fish.

Mr. Asa fed Major Powell and his men fresh fish, melons, and squash until they couldn't eat anymore. And what a well-deserved feast it was! Three months and more than a thousand miles after leaving Green River, the men had emerged from the great unknown.

But what of the others? Several scouts eventually brought the news. William Dunn and the Howland brothers were dead. They had been killed by a band of Shivwits Indians. It wasn't until Major Powell sat by a fire in a Shivwits camp almost a year later that he learned the full story. The Indians told him a group of prospectors had killed a Shivwits woman. A band of Shivwit braves mistook Dunn and the Howlands for the prospectors and killed them in revenge.

As for the rest of the crew, they scattered in different directions after their great feast at the Virgin River. Well-fed and supplied, George Bradley and Jack Sumner took one of the boats and rowed as far as Yuma, Arizona. Andy Hall and Billy Hawkins took the other and rowed it all the way to the Gulf of Mexico.

For Major Powell, there was no reason to go on. The lower river had already been explored. He and his brother Walter traveled out together and rode a train back East. But Major Powell would return.

In 1871, Powell led a second expedition down the Green and Colorado rivers. For many years to come, he continued to roam the rugged canyon country. He continued to record his observations of the rocks, plants, and animals of the region. He continued to learn the customs and languages of the native people who lived in these harsh lands. He continued his lifelong adventure—into the unknown.

For More Information

You can learn more about John Wesley Powell and his river adventures by writing or visiting the following places:

John Wesley Powell Memorial Museum
6 North Lake Powell Boulevard
P.O. Box 547
Page, AZ 86040
(602) 645-9496

John Wesley Powell River History Museum
885 East Main Street
Green River, UT 84525
(801) 564-3427

Grand Canyon National Park
P.O. Box 129
Grand Canyon, AZ 86023
(602) 638-7888